8 Keys to Master Barbering

Unlock the Doors that Lead to Success

Andre Moore

ClearVision Publishing
Nashville, Tennessee

First Edition

Library of Congress Catalog Publication Data
ISBN: 978-0-578-04217-6

Published by ClearVision Publishing, Nashville, TN

Design and layout by Proctor Solutions

Edited by PAGE Communications and the Xlibris Corporation

Printed in the United States of America

To my loving wife, my children, and the clients that stuck around long enough to see our way of doing business become a standard for the industry.

About the Author

Andre Moore has ten years of field experience. He is the owner of Cuttin'-It-Close Barber and Beauty and is a member of the Barbers' Inner Circle. He received his bachelor's degree in economics and finance from Tennessee State University and worked in marketing for a Fortune 500 company.

His Favorite Quote

> "If you're doing something you care deeply about and truly believe in, it's impossible to invest in it fully and not become great."

A Word from the Author

Over the years, I've learned a lot—mostly the hard way. Because of this, I put time into writing this book to help you avoid the many obstacles I had to struggle through. This book is more than advice, tips, and information put to ink and paper. It's a lifetime of friends, influences, and experiences that have touched my heart in some special way. This book is the cleansing of my experiences and understanding told in a straightforward way. If you are serious about becoming a top-rated master barber or stylist, you will enjoy this book.

Contents

Preface

They can't keep hiding the keys!

In this life, there are many uncertainties; fortunately for barbers and stylists, there is one thing that is definite—hair. There will never be a shortage of hair. As long as the sun continues to rise on an earth full of people, barbers and stylists will have opportunities to make money. The question is, "How can we turn these opportunities into successful careers?"

Let's face it, all barber-stylists eventually become good, but only a few actually advance to great. We all know many good barbers and stylists who never seem to quite reach full potential. The *8 Keys to Master Barbering* is written to help barbers and beauticians obtain key but often overlooked business principles that frequently appear as an illusion in some unobtainable fantasyland. This book is *not* written to teach new styles nor does it contain the latest techniques. The harsh reality is that in barber and/or beauty school, only approximately 3.6 percent[1] of studies go toward learning the business skills actually needed not only to separate leaders from the competition in an already congested industry but more importantly to launch successful careers.

Since you are reading this book, you have taken the first step toward unlocking the doors that lead not only to success but also to a successful career. Specifically, the *8 Keys to Master Barbering* is written to show how your skills help boost the confidence of everyday people as well as to show how intertwining your clientele's talents make for the good of the shop. The eight keys will also demonstrate how the cosmetology industry enhances the local economy. As you can see, the *8 Keys to Master Barbering* will cover several areas that lead toward triumphant careers. Various keys such as keeping a clean shop and being on time may seem simple, but the book will show how these keys are the foundations that really reflect you. As

---

1. Based on the number of pages in *Milady's Standard Textbook of Professional Barber-Styling* that are not business principles pages (527 pages) divided by the number of pages (21 pages) in the textbook that are dedicated to business principles.

the book moves forward, it will also show how each key is the initial means for separating oneself from others. A few of the other keys the book focuses on are why it's important to sell the best products, keeping up with the latest tools/trends, understanding taxes, and developing and maintaining a healthy budget. This book gives specific details to how budgets will help fund future opportunities and, at the same time, will show how to withstand unseen misfortunes that always seem to lurk around every corner.

In addition, the *8 Keys to Master Barbering* also contain examples of surveys that help get to the bottom of what consumers really crave. More than often, barbers and stylists, over time, become complacent and unaware of how to reel in new clients. This book aims to examine innovative methods for unlocking potential new business by observing traditional and nontraditional methods for marketing avenues. Once new business is gained, as shown in the fourth key, this book shifts focus to illustrate how to communicate with the captured new clients by using strategies based on today's technological tools. Basically, these eight keys are designed to unlock your potential. So are you prepared to go to the next level?

The *8 Keys to Master Barbering* is written to separate you from the pack. Let's face it, no matter how good we are, word of mouth only goes so far. Luck eventually runs out. This book lists step-by-step processes that will advance your career. You will wonder how you made it this far. Now let's go over the *8 Keys to Master Barbering* so you can apply them to your day-to-day operations.

Understand Your Place in the Community

Key 1

Know thyself.

Since knowledge is the key to power, understanding the *ins* and *outs* of any profession makes an individual an expert compared to others in the same industry. For this reason, barbers and stylists that acquire a holistic understanding of job responsibilities will better service clients and the community. "Knowledge is power" is a true statement in all professions. This is why some professionals experience *word-of-mouth* business and others do not. So professionals that consistently show a good understanding of their respected profession and provide more than is expected (to clients) will always experience an increasing customer base. Because of this, smart professionals separate themselves from the pack. This is especially true in the cosmetology field. To illustrate, a customer may experience something he has little knowledge about, like a furuncle (an acute bacterial infection of a hair follicle, producing pain). An expert barber-stylist will exonerate the client's furuncle and will also provide the client with information of what the causes of the client's problem are so that preventive actions are taken in the future. This client will leave a happier, more informed customer. Actually, what happened is the barber-stylist provided a boost of confidence. The reason—the hair bump is taken care of, but more importantly, the client's life is changed from the new information received because of the barber-stylist's vast knowledge.

In the example above, the barber-stylist understands who he/she is to the customer and, as a result, is able to empower the customer. This client will share his experience with others. Therefore, empowering customers empowers you—word of mouth travels. The more you know about your true purpose, the more opportunities you have to empower customers and expand your clientele.

Because of your expertise, clients will trust you in other areas as well. Part of your job is to communicate, and the most important part of communicating is listening. Be prepared to listen. I would say listening accounts for about 50 percent of a barber-stylist's job.[2] Customers will come into a welcoming atmosphere ready to talk. In essence, you will, over time, become a counselor for many of your clients. This is good for you because the cost of counseling is steadily rising. In current times, it is no secret that family and friends can't always be trusted and the costs of counseling sessions are at least about $95[3] an hour. That may not be expensive for some of your clients, but for most, $95 an hour eventually adds up. Yet people need to vent situations, big or small, that bound their lives. For this reason, barbers and stylists are becoming confidants for their clients.

---

2. Based on over ten years of experience.
3. Based on 2008 counseling costs from The Counseling Group, Brentwood, Tennessee.

We as barber-stylists must be trustworthy since clients often let us in on the secret areas of their lives: *I'm having a baby, I just left court, my spouse and I are going through rough times, I want to go back to school, my credit score is decreasing, I got laid off today* . . . Prepare yourself to listen to just about everything. The beauty, we do not have to give advice, but we are obliged to listen. Customers appreciate a listening ear and a shoulder to lean on. Regardless, prepare yourself to be a strong and unbiased sounding board; it will help you separate yourself from the crowd.

If you are a barber-stylist that is a good listener, you put yourself in the best position to help customers. There are advantages to listening to your customers. For one, you get to hear what their needs and desires are. An overlooked function of a barber-stylist is his or her ability to network for clients. Plus, in today's economy, who among us do not need help? Listening may seem like a small thing, but it can take barber-stylists further than you can imagine. We help immensely by simply paying attention. By listening, we can connect our customers' skills with other customers' needs. One of the great delights of a master barber-stylist is being surrounded by people that have trades and professions from all walks of life. Not only does everyone do something, every other person is looking for something. Believe me, leading barber-stylists make connections for clients that are looking for services with our clients that provide the same services. If your listening skills are attuned, clients will automatically tell you what is needed in their lives. Most of the time, ordinary barber-stylists miss what the client is saying because the barber-stylist does most of the talking. However, we all know that the most important part of communicating is listening. To illustrate, consider this scenario. While getting a hairstyle, your customer states that her computer is having system problems. Earlier that same day, you cut a guy's hair who works on computers in his spare time. This is perfect for you and both clients. For one, you cut two heads of hair, but you have also encountered two customers who can benefit from each other simply because you listened. In a situation like this, you are able to make two customers happy; one gets her computer fixed for a good price, and the other gets an opportunity to make extra cash.

Now cutting clients' hair helps them enhance their appearance, but networking on a client's behalf helps you in the long run. When clients realize that you have their best interest at heart, you have truly created a long-term relationship. If nothing else in this section connects, remember to always find ways to support what your customers are doing.

A more obvious service, provided by barbers and stylists, is giving consumer confidence. No matter how often I see it, I am still amazed to see a client leave with a boost of confidence just because he or she got a new hairstyle. The customer still has on the same attire but manages to leave with a *big* grin because of his or her new haircut.

A client of mine had an interview with a leading firm in the area. He spent a nice amount on a new suit and tie. He also bought and studied a book of most likely asked questions for interviews. It is safe to say that he wanted to leave a lasting impression on his interviewers. Regardless of all the preparation, he wanted to make sure his hair was trimmed right before the interview. He looked at his haircut as the final touch or the icing on the cake, one could say. No matter what the other provisions were, the glow on his face defined his strut after the addition of a haircut. The haircut gave him a shot of confidence. He left the shop more poised.

The reality is that a fresh style or clean cut provides confidence. Even though we cut and style hair, we have all even experienced that feeling ourselves. It is of most importance that we as barbers and stylists make sure that we see that *big* smile on the face of our customers before they leave our barbershops and beauty salons. Ultimately, this is how we get paid.

Getting paid is vital because money earned helps stimulate the local economy. Everything barbers and stylists do on a micro level helps clients; however, the summation of helping all clients fuels the local economy on a macro level. Understanding how we as barbers and stylists support the economy that surrounds us is extremely significant.

Our incomes help to stimulate cities' economies and growth overall. First of all, let's understand what's going on. Cities are formed to create economies of scale for large corporations, so most cities are large and have diverse collections of economic activity.[4] As a result, large labor pools are created to support thriving businesses. The companies' employees spend their income with local businesses: grocery stores, barbershops, hospitals, housing construction, beauty salons, sporting events, malls, etc. To summarize, employees make companies run. People work, eat,

---

4. Arthur O'Sullivan, *Urban Economics* (New York: McGraw-Hill/Irwin Publishing, 2003), 39.

sleep; work, eat, sleep; work, eat, sleep; and so on. For many, life can be redundant. Fortunately, barbershops and beauty salons not only provide service to the local economy, shops and salons also provide a sense of calmness in a hectic, ever-moving, fast-paced world. So the money earned by master barbers and stylists is in turn spent in other local businesses. As money is recycled from business to business, the local economy thrives. The cosmetology industry, like other local businesses, plays a vital role in stimulating positive growth in healthy economies.

As a master barber-stylist, your job responsibilities stretch beyond just providing a good hairstyle. For timeless success, provide consumer confidence, be a networking hub for your clients' talents, and learn to be a confidant. These extra attributes help stimulate the local economy as well. Many barber-stylists will not go the extra mile nor will they go above and beyond. This is great for you. Satisfaction in this industry is no different than in any other industry—

consumers will spend their dollars where they get more bang for their buck. Understand who you are, know what you are capable of, and you will be more than a professional; you will be one of the few professional experts in your industry.

Create the Right Atmosphere

Key 2

The customer's lenses are the only ones that count.

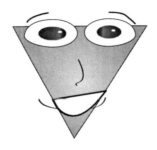

A shop's success depends on its atmosphere, the mood, or the impression it leaves on the minds of customers. In addition to the vibe—keeping a clean shop, selling the best products, and keeping up with latest tools and trends—are also very important aspects to creating the right atmosphere. Hopefully, this is no secret. The variables listed in the first key provide an internal view of what barbers and stylists think customers want. To really connect, surveys are needed to gain an external view to find out what customer desires are and to determine the direction of the market. Average

23

barbers and stylists hope customers return, but leaders dig deep to gain the internal and external information needed to service clients that happily return. To determine the right atmosphere, we must learn to listen and appreciate the customers' point of view.

Fortunately, there are many different atmospheres and/or themes that help differentiate barber and beauty shops all across the world: family-valued shops, sports-themed shops, urban shops, religious shops, trendy shops, hole-in-the-wall shops, and so on. No matter how the right atmosphere is defined, a shop's environment must be intriguing, appealing, and based on customer preferences. Shop owners must decide which atmospheres attract the most customers based on the location of the shop. More than often, shop owners do not capitalize entirely on profit margins because they fail to consider the best atmosphere for the location that their shop encompasses. For example, on Third Avenue and Trinity Lane, there is a shop that has six forty-two-inch wall-mounted flat-screen TVs. Throughout the day, all TVs stay fixed on channels that enable customers to keep real updates of the stock market, interest rates, and current economic indicators, and so on. Furniture and fixtures are also first-class choices. According to the shop owner, this shop has the right atmosphere. Unfortunately, this shop is in an area of town where investing in stocks or anything positive is not the top priority. Now this would have been a perfect shop if it were in the heart of downtown where lawyers, bankers, judges, and others interested in investing dominate the area. The shop failed as a business; it failed because the owner did not consider the customers' point of view.

It is very important that a shop's atmosphere corresponds with the environment. Once the right atmosphere is established, it must remain consistent through time. Establishing the right atmosphere now is very important for establishing baseline marketing strategies in later chapters. In key 4, "Always Increase Your Client Base," marketing methods will be discussed to help distinguish you from the crowd. Customers will support businesses where they feel at home. Solutions—create the right atmosphere and stand out as a distinct business in your area.

Besides the ideal environment, customers desire the best products. Because today's world is hectic and chaotic, buying top-shelf brands is one way for consumers to treat themselves to goodness in a harsh and busy world. The hair-care industry knows that people use products to boost confidence during these times. For this reason, the hair-care industry has grown a great deal. As a result, there is a vast amount of hair-care products that vary by different levels of quality, and the differences in product quality cause fluctuations in prices. Costs are very important to customers. They will pay for what is affordable. So it is very important that we stay committed to keeping the best products at the right prices our customers are willing to pay.

We all know that dandruff does not discriminate. Despite demographics, age, sex, or race, it affects all consumers. So it is important that we keep some sort of dandruff shampoo in our shops and salons. But we must be smart on what we stock based on our customers' preferences. We cannot stock a $65 dandruff shampoo (even though it may be the best brand on the market) in a shop that attracts lower-income customers. True, you may sell one or two bottles, but it is better to keep the best brand at the right price for the customer base each shop attracts. This way, a shop or salon can sell as many products as possible based on reasonable prices and respectable products. Keeping good products at comparable prices helps enhance the shop's environment.

Maintaining the latest tools and trends is not only expected, but it is also crucial for survival because technology and methods change every day. If we are expected to be leaders, we must accept change and reflect it by adjusting to innovations and by maintaining improved equipment. We must also adjust to or create newer, more contemporary styles. To keep pace or stay ahead, we must be informed. Yes, information is the key. To stay ahead of the information curve, action on your part is required. Stay updated by subscribing to industry magazines and newsletters. Attend hair shows and compete. Competing lets your customers know that you are on the cutting edge. If we do not take action and make room for change, we will slowly but surely trap ourselves with a dying clientele and old styles. Adding new styles increases clientele, and accumulating a new customer base on a regular basis is a must to survive.

Furthermore, adapting to change helps ensure continued existence. Remember the dinosaurs? They were not able to adapt to change. This is the opposite action of leaders. Leaders are innovators and pacesetters. Since not everyone is a trendsetter, one of the easier ways to separate from the pack is to keep up with the latest tools and trends. This simple act will make you a light in darkness, and consumers will flock to the light like a moth to a flame.

To create a pleasant environment, barbers and stylists must also take into consideration the image we reflect of ourselves in shops and salons. As respected professionals, we are in the spotlight more than we know, so we must sustain a high level of professionalism. What we wear is essential, how we connect to diverse groups is crucial, and since barbershops and beauty salons strive to provide services for all family members, we must also stay sober. Basically, wearing unprofessional clothes only attracts certain people, plus drinking alcohol and/or doing drugs creates bad vibes and therefore is disrespectful to clients. You may be able to get away with this behavior with a few clients, but be assured you will run off the rest. Even if you are the best barber-stylist within your community, your skills will become insignificant if there are no heads left to cut or style. Believe me, people do not need many excuses to spend money elsewhere, so customers constantly watch to see if we maintain a level of professionalism at all times.

No matter how much you spend trying to create the right atmosphere, recognize that you are one of the main ingredients for the success of your shop's environment. Take pride in yourself as much as you do in your skills.

The final key to creating the right environment is finding out for certain what customers actually crave. Leaders are awarded for seeking and implementing customers' specific needs. A good way to find out what customers want is to create and implement surveys for potential customers. Creating surveys ensures a thorough understanding of the marketplace, which then enables leaders to lead with the correct trends of the future.[5] To grow a business, recognizing what customers look for and responding to those needs create the right environment. Collecting data is a step in the right direction toward increasing clientele. Although

---

5. Steven S. Little, *The 7 Irrefutable Rules of Small Business Growth* (Hoboken: John Wiley & Son Publishing, 2005).

there is no exact science to collecting data, I have listed a few points to follow (see figure 1):

- At least thirty questionnaires are needed to get a good sample of a specific population.
- Develop your survey with the end in mind.
- Try not to have too many questions—no more than fifteen.
- Tie questions to the scope of your research—if questions don't tie to scope, delete.
- Data collection or gathering methods: Web, telephone, face-to-face interview, text message.

It is not by chance that successful shops always have great atmospheres. The owners simply had good ideas that were implanted correctly. BREAKING NEWS: their ideas are no better than yours. Follow the steps considered necessary to create an incredible setting in your own shop:

1. Create an appealing experience at your shop by valuing your customers' point of view. This way, you and your shop will stand out.
2. Sell the best products and brands at the right price.
3. Never become complacent; always adjust when innovations are introduced.
4. Always remember to present *you* in a professional manner.

31

Figure 1

Survey Questions

1. What is your age group?

   _____ 18–20   _____ 21–25

   _____ 26–30   _____ 31–40

2. What is your gender?

   _____ M   _____ F

3. How often do you go out?

   _____ More than once a week   _____ Once a week

   _____ Twice a month   _____ Once a month

   _____ Almost never

4. What do you enjoy most about going out?

5. Do you like sports?

   _____ Y   _____ N

6. How likely are you to attend a sports bar?

   _____ Very likely   _____ Likely

   _____ Almost never   _____ Never

7. If you do not attend sports bars, why not?

8. Do you feel that local sports bars embrace your culture/community?

   _____ Yes   _____ Sometimes   _____ Never

9. What is the **most important** dining element in a sports bar?

Be Forthcoming with Clientele

Key 3

Honesty is the best policy.

Let's get one thing straight: happy customers are paying customers, and paying customers are returning customers. Nowadays it is impossible to have a thriving business with unhappy customers. Let's face it, customers have become very savvy and are more demanding than ever. To stay alive, pleasing customers is very important. Yes, the cosmetology industry is in the business of providing confidence; however, there are many ways to please customers other than providing a great haircut or style. Customers want more. Being up-front and honest is one of the more crucial ways to keep customers happy. It's time-out for us taking our customers for granted. Like all respectable businesses, barbershops and salons need to convey realistic business hours and actual days of operations with clients. If we expect clients to continue to return, we have to respect them and realize that honesty builds trust. Trust is an important element for all relationships. As long as we are open and candid with clients about endeavors that may pull us away from regular business hours, they will return. We want customers that stay with us over time. A trusted book even says that truth withstands the test of time (Proverbs 12:19, NLT).

One thing we cannot get back is lost time. So being on time is extremely important. Barbers and stylists must learn to begin work no later than the time communicated to customers. This is true for all professionals that expect to make more than the average competitor. This statement includes us as well. I hate to sound redundant, but barbers and stylists have to be on time too.

We must open doors consistently at the same time each workday. Does this mean we all have to be at work at 8:00 a.m. every day? No, but if shop hours are 8:00 a.m. to 6:00 p.m., we must honor the business hours we have set. If business hours begin at 10:00 a.m., doors need to be open by

10:00 a.m., not 1:00 p.m., noon, 11:15 a.m., or 10:30 a.m. Inconsistency is the easiest way to lose customers. I had a barber who used to cut my hair that came in whenever he pleased. He was an exceptional barber; I mean, the guy was nice with clippers, but my time was too valuable to waste. It didn't take long for me to find another barber. I'm sure we all have similar testimonies. The bottom line is that I felt that my time was not valued. As far as I know, no one wants to be disrespected. Showing up for work when it best suits you is disrespectful, unacceptable, and will not be tolerated for long.

Of course, things do happen where we cannot always be on time. For the most part, we know when these outside obligations will delay us from being on time. These reasons for being late are okay *if* the explanations are well communicated in advance. Communicate new times with customers one way or the other: put flyers on your mirrors, use sticky notes, send e-mails, send text messages, and call customers when necessary. Always try to let clients know of time changes in advance. This way, they can make adjustments. This small act of concern for others' time will keep your clients happy.

What is inexcusable is tardiness due to laziness. If it gets in the way of your business, do not hang out all night. Have a life, but do not do it at the expense of your customer's time. Keep in mind, somewhere there is a barber or stylist who always makes it to work on time. It is just a matter of time before your clients find their way to them. Customers know that things happen, situations arise, and issues come up. They know you may not always be able to show up on time; just let them know when these circumstances occur. In return, they will respect your honesty and reward you by adjusting their schedules to what's going on in your life.

Now being constantly late is one problem, but barbers and stylists that skip days, I mean days that have been relayed as workdays, is even worse. NEWS FLASH: Set your days to work and honor them. It is important to open on days relayed to customers because they come in based on events that surround their lives. They will go to work, concerts, or interviews with an outdated perm or an overdue haircut only so many times. Reality check: barbers and stylists that skip entire workdays are selfish and/or self-centered. You know the type—Mr. or Ms. Egotistical. The person who is only concerned with one's own self. If this is you (egotistical), do not expect to have customers for long.

Ageless customers expect barbers and stylists to keep an honest business schedule. If Mondays and Tuesdays are unproductive days and you would rather do something else, just set your days of operation Wednesdays through Saturdays. Customers will not be offended that you do not work on Mondays and Tuesdays; actually, they will be happy to know your true work schedule. The bottom line, be honest with customers and communicate actual workdays. Do not lose customers on such a basic but sound principle—keep your customers informed.

Always Increase

Client Base

Key 4

More is better!

In any healthy system, circulation is needed to maintain balance. Like light and darkness or the yin and yang, things of opposite attraction need each other to remain in balance. A certain amount of circulation is always needed. According to the *Merriam-Webster Dictionary*, *circulate* means to move in a circular motion, circuit, or an orbit. To illustrate, try not breathing for twenty minutes. Yeah, air must flow freely *in* and *out* of the human body. No one can just "have air" to survive; it must be inhaled and exhaled. Quite frankly, in most cases, circulation is a necessity. Look at banks. Banks do not just have money coming *in*. Banks must also lend money *out* through personal loans, lines of credit for small businesses, and/or provide mortgages to survive.[6] For barbers and stylists, clients are the lifeline of business. Having clients is great, but eventually some leave. It's inevitable. So it is important to know how to attract new customers on a regular basis to maintain a healthy balance for your clientele to stay stable. What is unhealthy is having more clients leaving to spend money elsewhere than coming back to patronize your business. To stay balanced, traditional and nontraditional methods of increasing clientele must not only be explored but also implemented on a regular basis.

There are many traditional methods used to highlight business. An illustration is business cards. Passing out business cards is a conventional yet almost effortless method for increasing clientele. Even though business cards can be simple and effortless methods for letting potential customers know what you do, specific details should not be overlooked. First, make sure your card is an eye-

---

6. Rudiger Dornbusch, Stanley Fischer, and Richard Startz, *Macroeconomics* (New York: McGraw-Hill/Irwin Publishing, 2001), 381.

catcher. Since a business card may be a potential client's first visual (for your business), put a lot of thought into creating a lasting first impression. Here are a few examples.

Figure 2

Business Card Examples

To create a distinctive look for your business cards, there are many software programs such as Adobe Illustrator. On the other hand, if you are not a great artist but have great ideas for unique business cards, there are companies that specialize in photographic art such as Roland's Photography

41

(www.rolandsphotography.net) and Proctor Solutions (www.proctorsolutions.com). There are many companies that specialize in graphic capabilities. These unique companies can create just about anything you can imagine. Whatever you do, do not waste time copying business card styles that are seen everywhere. Create business cards you will love to pass out. Make sure they have a *wow* factor. This will give potential clients the idea that you have the *wow* factor when it comes to styling and cutting abilities as well. Although passing out business cards is a common method used by most barbers and stylists for gaining new business, your cards should not be ordinary unless you and your abilities are average. Make sure your business card approach reflects you, your style, and your character. This way, your business cards will become a great first line for attracting and increasing your client base.

Once you get amazing business cards, pass them out everywhere you go and with all transitions: mall purchasers, people in the mall, restaurant servers, people dining in restaurants, bank tellers, people in banks, hardware assistants, churchgoers, etc. More than anything, do not just be proud of your cards; make them totally work for you. Make them reach people you have never met. Send your business cards out with bills . . . every month.[7] Potential clients will be impressed with your persistence.

Also, when you receive business cards in passing or from other businesses you may have patronized, send them handwritten thank-you letters at the end of each month. Miss no opportunities. As a matter of fact, send business cards out with any and all mail that is sent out. I am sure you realize everyone will not do this. As you begin to figure more innovative ways to get your business cards into the hands of potential clients, watch how quickly you separate yourself from others in the barber and stylist world that surrounds your area.

---

7. Tom Hopkins, *How to Master the Art of Selling* (New York: Warner Books Edition, 1982), 242.

In this industry, you will also quickly learn that business comes in cycles. Eventually you will be able to predict downtime as clear as weathermen predict conditions for upcoming days. Barbers and/or stylists need to recognize these times because downtimes are potential gold mines.[8]

Since downtime is expected and should be recognized, ambitious barbers and stylists can use the otherwise leisurely time more efficiently by attacking nontraditional doors to unlock new business opportunities. Funeral homes, local county jails, retirement homes, mental health establishments, and more are neglected prospects for additional business prospects.

After targeting the best opportunities for your demographics, discount prices lower than regular style and fade prices to gain bulk opportunities. Think win, win. If your price is low, they win and you win because new business is gained in what would otherwise have been downtime. For instance, if you usually charge $15 for a regular

---

8. Take advantage of downtime. I wrote this book in mine!

fade, you may want to charge about $9 as a discount. I know, I know. *Why would I lose $6?* Companies may not be able to afford regular prices when several customers need service. Do not worry about the lost $6; think big. If the business has fifty potential clients, you can make an additional $450[9] to add to your weekly profits. Now if you can find new business once a week in any of the other nontraditional prospects, you can increase your monthly profits by $1,800 and yearly profits by $21,600. So consider losing $21,600 when you turn down business over six bucks by avoiding discounting to gain bulk opportunities. Also, work out and/or understand the company's method of paying you from the beginning. This will keep you from getting frustrated. Always think about the big picture. If you do not, someone more determined and eager will. That's a fact.

Since a few customers will always leave, make sure to always use traditional and nontraditional methods to continuously increase your client base.

---

9. 50 clients x $9 = $450.

There cannot be a ying without a yang, and people cannot live without inhaling *and* exhaling. Circulation is a necessity. Always keep the circulation of your clientele healthy and balanced. In the cosmetology industry, clients are the lifeline of business. We must accept the fact that some clients eventually leave for services elsewhere. So work hard to make sure new clients always enter your establishment.

Keep Open Communication

Key 5

Can you hear me now?

Savvy business leaders always find ways to communicate with clients. Whether (if it's) radio commercials, newspaper announcements, or bus-stop seating signs, marketing teams are constantly getting their messages across to the masses. Communication is very important. Large corporations such as Coca-Cola spend millions of dollars a year to speak to customers through sophisticated marketing campaigns. With proper planning, small businesses can also compete for clients by taking advantage of undersized but efficient marketing plans (key 6). With so many companies out for the same dollar, smart businesses know that they have to communicate how and why there are differences between your business and competitors.

We are fortunate to live in the world with many ways to get messages across to the masses. With new technology at the fingertips of everyone's hand and the traditional correspondent methods of yesterday, you will wonder why all businesses do not at least communicate with internal customers. To communicate with external potential customers, mass media provides several avenues. Mass media has pros and cons that must also be considered when creating a good communication plan. No matter the method, communication is a subject that must be looked at closer.

New Technological Methods of Communication

Technology has opened a new world and flattened the playing field for small business owners. The ability to communicate does not have to be dominated by the Fortune 500 firms anymore. This is great news for all barbers and stylists. To be specific, if you have a cell phone and/or Internet access, you have the basic tools considered necessary to communicate to your customers. New technology such as cell phones and Internet access gives barbers and stylists the ability to speak to large groups of people with text messaging and e-mail blasts. The good thing about both of these methods is that they are both virtually free! Texting and e-mail blasts are often overlooked but should be commonly used tools by all barbers and stylists. These technological tools will allow barbers and stylists to send daily, weekly, monthly, or quarterly messages to hundreds of people on a regular basis. Send business hours that may have changed, send price cuts or sells that you and your shop may have, or send results of in-shop polls. Frankly, send any type of message that you can think of to stay on your clients' minds. Remember, not many will use these tools, so doing either one will easily help propel your career.

By sending a few words, customers will be pleased about your efforts to keep in touch with them. Customer contact information is very important. If you do not have the cell numbers and e-mail addresses of your clients, create a drawing for a free haircut or style in exchange for the information needed. In other words, have customers put their full contact information on a card (see fig. 3) into a fishbowl (or something) and pick a winner for one of your best services.

Figure 3

Clipper Creations	
INFO CARD	
PRIZE: **$50.00 FREE SERVICE** (*In-house*)	
Name:	_____
Address:	_____
	_____
E-mail:	_____
Cell Phone:	_____

This small giveaway will allow you to gain the information needed to keep in touch with your customers for the cost of just a haircut, style, or color treatment. Now once you get your clients' personal information, do not send or forward junk mail, jokes, comical or biblical quotes to your customers. Only inform customers of business and shop issues. If you send any other type of mail, your customers will begin to delete your e-mails and/or texts before they even open the ones that you perceive as important. We all remember the story of the boy who cried wolf (unnecessarily). The boy tricked his peers into thinking he needed help so many times that when he really needed help, no one came to his defense. Do not cry wolf; don't waste people's time. Only send texts and e-mails of substance. Send information like updates, shop news, or price cuts at least once a quarter but more frequently preferably. This way, your customers will look forward to your communications.

Besides text messaging and e-mail blasts, Web sites are also effective technological tools. It may be more costly but provides an opportunity for you to reach out of the scope of the original clients you already have. This is why a Web site is one of the Internet's wealthiest resources. It has the ability to inform customers of you and your business on a global perspective. The Internet has millions of users every day. With such a tremendous amount of customers, you are sure to gain new clients or at least make more people aware of you and your distinct style. Web sites should be created to engage viewers of your diverse techniques. Visuals, sound, and movement are Web page advantages. Viewers can see your latest styles, print coupons for your promotions, view the products you sell, and even buy some online. They can also read through your history, view photos of current styles, and photos of your involvement in community events. A Web site can even put a unique spin on directions to your shop or salon.

There are so many things a Web site can do. I highly recommend getting on the Internet even if it's something like Facebook. You have to build a nice informative interface. There are many Web design companies. Take your time when choosing a good Web site company. A good example is proctersolutions.com. If possible, make sure the company you choose creates a sign-in page for new viewers so that you can get the new viewer's e-mail information to add to your e-mail blast list. Because a Web site does so much, it is a great form of communication. It is, to say the least, an attention grabber, which overtime adds awareness of you and improves your client base.

Traditional Methods of Communication

Technology has enhanced many forms of communication; however, it is not the only way to reach consumers. Methods may have changed, but reaching out to customers is nothing new. Communication has been entangled within the strategies of business since the beginning of (business) time. Think about it. In the early years of Sears' dominance, it was able to emerge as a leader in its industry by deploying aggressive marketing strategies. They mailed catalogs to thousands of customers instead of waiting for them to come into the store. Before technology made its mark in marketing communications, marketing was dominated by mailing postcards, informative letters, and phone calls. While these methods seem ancient, there are occasions when a touch of old-school communication is still effective.

Traditional methods of communication give customers a sense of personal touch that is missing in technical methods of communication. What's this got to do with you, right? A sense of personal touch is still needed in today's crazy, fast-paced world. It is needed because life will always deal people with *ups* and *downs*. We all go through highs and lows. These positive and negative situations give barbers and stylists opportunities to add personal touches to clients' lives.

One year I sent out "Happy Holidays" postcards in the beginning of December. On the postcard, I simply provided times of operation for the holidays and wrote, "God bless you and your family over the holidays. Be safe and see you soon." The response was overwhelming! At that time, we had the smallest shop on our side of town. Sending the postcards enhanced our clients' lives, and as a result, we had the busiest shop (on our side of town) by far. Think about it; most people check the mail and only receive bills or junk mail. Our customers were happy and surprised to receive a postcard from our shop. Such a simple act got a great response. Plus, sending postcards is very inexpensive. After Christmas, I suggest that you buy some postcards because they are usually on sale for significant discounts afterward. As a matter of fact, buy all cards when they are out of season. Besides holiday cards, "Thank You" and "Congratulations" cards should also be sent to customers to help them celebrate life's ups. To get even more personal, send letters for different occasions or events. See figure 1.4 for an example of an informative letter sent for a summer holiday. Try it! You will be surprised to see how far this type of personal touch goes.

As for the downs, we all know that life is not always glamorous or wonderful. There are times when your customers will experience painful and uncomfortable situations. Because of your listening ear, you will know when these times occur. Your clients vent all kinds of situations to you since you have created a trusting relationship between you and your client (see key 1). "My son just got out of the hospital. He broke his arm." "My wife was in a car wreck." "My father died yesterday." "I was laid off from my job yesterday." These situations are numbing and tough times for clients. Not only must barbers and stylists reach out on positive times of our clients' lives, we must also reach out when negative circumstances occur too. We must call or send sympathy cards to our clients to let them know that they and their situations are in our prayers. We must call or send sympathy cards to let them know that we are sorry for their loss. We need to call or send sympathy cards to let them know we hope they get well soon. And so on. A phone call and a sympathy card are both effortless but very personal. As long as we are sincere and genuine, our intentions will be felt from the heart and will go a long way. As a matter of fact, barbers and stylists that provide personal touches of comfort to their clients' lives will always experience heartfelt growth.

Figure 4

CUTTIN'-It-CLOSE Barber & Beauty

(615) 650-7570–1212 Dickerson Road
Nashville TN 37290

August 23, 2004

The summer has come to an end and Labor Day weekend may be your last chance to barbecue this season! Do not let us stand in the way. The shop will **open at 7:00 a.m.** this Saturday so that you may have more time to burn up the grill or anything else you may have planned.

Here are a few sites to find great, quick and easy recipes for the grill.

http://www.barbecuen.com/
http://barbecue.allrecipes.com/
http://www.recipeland.com.8080/search/?q=barbeque
&si=contains

Holidays can be dangerous; please close the summer on a safe note.

See you soon,
CIC Management

Mass Media Methods for Communication

To savvy businesspersons, there are two types of people: those that you already know (internal) and those that you have yet to meet (external). So far, communication has been viewed as a tool used to connect with internal customers. To communicate with external consumers, mass media (see fig. 1.5) is often used to bring awareness to you and/or your business.

No matter if it is radio ads, television commercials, or newspaper articles, mass media is used to market most businesses. In most cases, yearlong marketing plans are created. Stretching a marketing plan over a long duration of time ensures that your message reaches prospective customers. A good plan will usually entail at least one or will have a combination of more than one of the advertising media: radio, cable, newspaper, magazines, direct mail, or a couple of other avenues. As with anything, there are pros and cons. The strength of using mass media—each avenue reaches large amounts of people. The one deterrent—high costs. Because media costs can be expensive, promotion decisions must be made carefully using a systematic approach.[10] What audience are you attracting? How much capital is set aside for marketing? Which combination will permit at least a year's worth of marketing? All types of questions must be considered to get the right marketing mixture for success.

Figure 5

Advertising Media	_Advantage_
Radio commercials	Segmented audiences
Cable commercials	Sight, sound, motion
Newspaper articles/ads	Ads can reach customers quickly and change as quickly
Magazine articles/ads	Targeted specific audiences
Direct mail	Personal messages
Movie ads	Precise audiences
Festival/fair booths	Culture-targeted audiences

---

10. Eric Berkowitz et al., _Marketing_ (New York: McGraw-Hill/Irwin Publishing, 2003).

Since media costs can add up quickly, be sure to choose an avenue of mass media that fits within your budget. At the beginning, purchase cheaper ads. For example, if you choose the radio to communicate externally, the most listened to AM station may be the best option in the beginning stages of your marketing plan. An AM radio station needs advertisers as much as we need them. It is a fact that most radio stations have companies fighting over time slots during peak hours. We have to be smart though. Radio stations also have late-night time slots that have no commercials. Figure out the void slots from the radio station and buy blocks of that time. The AM station will probably sell the blocks of time at a discounted rate too; the radio stations need sales to survive. They would rather make some sort of profit for otherwise dead time slots than make no money at all during those times. You may have chosen odd hours, but you will eventually get positive feedback from the commercials. Take the profits from new clients and begin the same process on one of the more popular FM radio stations in your area. This approach can be used for any of the media avenues. Radio ads, cable commercials, newspaper ads/articles, magazines ads/articles, direct mail, movie ads, or festival booths can work to your advantage as long as a budget (key 8) is followed. Most barbers or stylists will never use mass media. Use this tool; it is a sure way for making yourself known to external potential customers.

Communication is an unwritten requirement that must be addressed. No matter if you use the technological message method, old-fashioned correspondence, or mass media, communication with clients is critical. Plan, budget, and take advantage of marketing plans.

Develop a Marketing Plan

Key 6

Do they know who you are?

How far can you get if you have no idea where you are going? Let's say that vacation time has come around again. The first thing you do is fill up the car; next you gather loved ones for an out-of-town trip. Your plans are simple—have a *great* time! You are so excited to be vacationing that you and the crew jump in the car with no regard for direction. You just drive. You drive until you run out of gas in hopes of having fun wherever you stop. You end up in the middle of nowhere. Unfortunately, a theme park was in a city four hours back. You realize that you have not only wasted money, you have also wasted time. This could have been avoided with a little preparation. I know this is an extreme illustration, but mapping out a destination is a key element to arriving at success.

Plotting a destination always helps save money and time. No one wants to be lost. One of the worse things a person can do is wander in the wilderness with no beginning or ending. Just like going out of town, it is always wise to have a plan and a map. A map helps guide you to your final destination as a well thought-out plan can help one accomplish goals. A marketing plan is similar to a map and a plan. Developing a marketing plan is important for barbers and stylists because it strategically shows how to gain and grow new clients. A marketing plan provides a detailed path of how and when to use the avenues discussed in key 5. A marketing plan is a road map for the marketing activities of an organization for a specified future time, such as one year or five years.[11] Since there are so many ways to communicate with internal and external customers (key 5), barbers and stylists need to tailor a marketing plan that specifically addresses his or her

---

11. Eric Berkowitz et al., *Marketing* (New York: McGraw-Hill/Irwin Publishing, 2003).

demographics and needs. Normally, a healthy marketing plan is created in three phases: the planning phase, the implementation phase, and the control phase. As we move forward, you will see how these three steps radically simplify the creation process of developing a marketing plan.

The Planning Phase

Whenever I have to look at myself for solutions, it's never an easy task. This is exactly what happens in the planning phase of marketing groundwork. It is difficult because it calls for self-reflection. We not only have to look at what we do well, but we must also identify areas of improvement. For this, we will use a SWOT analysis. We can evaluate our shops, salons, or ourselves with a SWOT analysis tool. A SWOT analysis describes your (or your company's) internal strengths and weaknesses and your external opportunities and threats. In figure 6, fill in the blanks of the SWOT analysis to see where you are internally (strengths and weaknesses) and externally (opportunities and threats) so you can see what skills you have that are worthy of highlighting and which areas need to be improved upon compared to others. For each box, list what you have or what you may need.

Figure 6

SWOT Analysis		
Internal Factors	**Strengths**	**Weaknesses**
Management		
Offerings		
Marketing		
Personnel		
Finance		
External Factors	**Opportunities**	**Threats**
Consumer		
Competitive		
Technological		
Economic		
Legal Aspect		

Once we figure out our strengths, weaknesses, opportunities, and threats, we can do the following:

❖ *Determine industry trends (past and current).*
   What are barbers or beauticians doing successfully
   in your community? What have they done
   successfully in the past? Do your competitors
   reach out to customers through mass media,
   Internet? Have they in the past? Do my skills,
   vision, or finances allow me to do what is being
   done successfully? Can the industry trend be an
   opportunity for me? Is it a weakness for me?

❖ *Analyze competitors.* Who are you competing with
   for customers? What differences are there between
   them and you? What do competitors do well
   (these are your threats)? What are their
   weaknesses (these are your opportunities)?

❖ *Assess ourselves or our companies (compared to
   competitors).* Based on the SWOT, what do you
   do better than competitors? How can you use your
   strengths to push the industry forward?

❖ *Research customers.* Based on what you do well,
   what kind of customers will best appreciate your
   strengths? These are the customers you should
   focus all efforts toward moving forward.

Analyzing these four points helps to identify gaps
among other barbers and beauticians in your area

and you. Once gaps are identified, exploit competitors' weaknesses by setting marketing goals that highlight your strengths and take advantage of opportunities.

Another advantage for looking at these four points is it helps you focus on your strengths and opportunities. What you do not want to do is set marketing goals to reach customers that highlight your weaknesses. I know this sounds crazy, but if you skip this exercise, you may think you do something well but the SWOT may reveal that compared to other barbers and stylists in the industry, you may not do what you think you do as well as you thought. If this is the case, customers will eventually become clients of your competitors on your marketing plan's behalf. Going through this exercise helps ensure that time and money invested highlights you, not your competitors. Also, competitors that do not read this book will probably draw attention to your strengths.

Focus your marketing plan by setting goals based on industry gaps and your strengths. Select target markets and customers that your services best highlight based on the points of difference the SWOT reveals. Position yourself based on differences. Highlight your strengths but also attack what threatens your competitors' business; attack their weaknesses. This does not mean to make your advertisements down talking your competitors' weaknesses. Instead, highlight what you definitely do well; at the same time, make sure it is something that you know the competition does not do so well.

After completing the SWOT analysis and figuring out how to market yourself, develop your program's marketing mix based on media elements chosen in key 5. Next, create a budget by estimating profits. In other words, use a percentage of your annual profits for your marketing plan. So if you make $3,000 a month, you can use 20 percent for marketing funds: $600 per month. At this rate, you can estimate that you will have about $7,200 ($600 × 12 months) marketing dollars for the year. Play around with the percentage until you come up with numbers that you are comfortable with investing toward a marketing plan. Use the final estimate to create a marketing plan for the year.

The Implementation Phase

Of your marketing plan, the implementation phase should be the easiest stage. In this phase, you have to assign responsibilities for actions and deadlines. Because this phase brings the planning phase to life, you have to make sure assignments are accomplished. The key here is to surround yourself with people that get things done. This is not the time to lean on friends that are procrastinators. If you plan to be successful in the implementation phase, do not let procrastinators take any part of this phase.

The implementation phase is said to be the easiest stage because you only have to make sure that assignments are completed. For each step, follow a system of chronological processes that must be completed. Processes ensure that people have routine methods for completing tasks. This will ensure that people meet deadlines. Even qualified people can miss deadlines if adequate processes are not in order. Always remember, a high percentage of the time, maybe 95 percent or more, people are never the problem. A lack of processes for qualified people to follow is most often the problem. A lack of processes will make this stage much more difficult than it should be. So after choosing qualified people, make sure you provide processes for them to follow.

Now that you have chosen the right people, the next steps in the implementation phase are to design a marketing organization and to develop schedules. When designing your marketing organization, you may have to insert your name in most of the responsibilities in the beginning until you grow to the point where you can afford to pay others. This way, you know exactly what needs to be done. After names have been inserted (mostly yours) into key roles, develop a time line to ensure that things are done in a timely manner.

After making sure processes, people, and schedules are in place, resources will fuel the implementation phase. Resources are the final ingredients needed in the implementation phase. People and processes are nothing without money. Obtaining proper resources is necessary for moving forward. Regardless if you save the money needed, get a loan from a friend, investment group, or bank, do not get caught without a plan to get the funds needed to fuel your marketing plan.

What if you put together a marketing plan that requires a $15,000 investment? In turn, this investment is expected to produce two hundred new clients. That would be a great plan but terrible if you have no initial start-up money to move forward on capturing two hundred new potential clients. If no money is saved, you have to go other routes. Your marketing plan must be presented to the right person or group. Typically, people or groups are more willing to invest in projects where the originator of the idea is as willing to invest in the idea as well. This means they need to see that you are willing to risk your money as well. No matter the situation, money, people, processes, timeliness, and organizing responsibilities are key elements for successfully implementing your marketing plan.

The Control Phase

Now that everything is intact, the last phase of executing your marketing program is to make sure controls are in place to ensure success. As actions are executed in the implantation phase, you can control the outcomes by assigning responsibilities to someone to gather data to see how good the plan is doing compared to the original plan. The control phase will point out problems and show what you are doing well.

Most people avoid this step and, as a result, are unaware of situations that should be corrected until it is too late. When is it too late? If customers are complaining, it's too late. The control phase will help you stay on track and correct problems if needed as they occur or to exploit opportunities immediately as they are discovered. So the controller's responsibilities would be to compare results of the original plan to actual executed items, which would identify deviations and would allow you to act quickly toward correcting negative deviations and exploit positive ones. Here are a few guidelines for your controller to follow:

- *Set measurable, achievable goals.* I want to increase x from 17 percent to 22 percent.
- *Use facts and valid assumptions.* It takes out uncertainties and reduces risks.
- *Keep it simple.* Good execution comes from clarity.

Most people do not plan to fail; they fail to plan. The planning phase, implementation phase, and control phase are all designed to help you execute your marketing plan to perfection. There is no reason to wander in the wilderness. A marketing plan will separate wise barbers and stylists from others. A well thought-out and executed marketing plan will enlarge your client base. Make sure you take the time to tailor a marketing plan that specifically addresses your growth potential.

Manage Your Money

Key 7

Managing money is an art.

Art can be expressed in many ways: paintings, drawings, music, literature, dance, and much more. Even a creative style from a barber or beautician is considered art (I hope you think of yourself as an artist; remember that beauty is in the eye of the beholder). Believe it or not, managing money can also be regarded as an art. If you do not believe me, ask a financial asset manager. However, managing money isn't easy for everyone. To some, managing money can be seen as a beautiful thing, to others, a catastrophe. For most entrepreneurs, managing money is one of the harder lessons to learn. Being endowed with an entrepreneurial spirit does not necessarily mean that entrepreneurs will be automatically equipped with a financial management tool kit. Unfortunately, mismanaging money does not exclude barbers and beauticians.

Even the best artists are trained, and fortunately, money management is an art that can be mastered through training as well.

With today's economic problems—increasing gas prices, groceries steadily rising, the demanding costs of health care, and everything else that is constantly escalating—managing money has become a hot topic. Who has not seen the endless amount of wealth-renovation paperbacks at the bookstores? *Financial Peace, The Millionaire Mind, The Total Money Makeover, Rich Dad, Poor Dad* . . . The list goes on. The reason there are so many books in this area is simple—attention needs to be given to managing money. Let's face it; managing finances is not everyone's cup of tea. Do not worry, the *8 Keys to Master Barbering* has identified two areas of finance that can help any entrepreneur better manage money: paying taxes and budgeting money. Paying taxes ensures that we are compliant with the law, and creating a budget ensures that the financial arrangements needed to reach success are in place to accomplish future goals.

Understand and Pay Taxes

I know, I know. Paying taxes is a headache for most people around the first of the year and is a pain for barbers and stylists as well. Taxes are so complicated that university law schools offer master's degrees in taxation to lawyers, many of whom are also certified public accountants.[12] CPAs know the ins and outs of accounting laws and changes. It's good to know one. According to CPA Ms. Dimeta Smith,[13] most independent contractors like barbers and beauticians are fearful of paying taxes because they just do not understand the tax system.

The tax system is set up to help fund educational programs, highways, and health care. Tax incentives also help keep jobs in the United States instead of sending them offshore. Even

---

12. Eugene Brigham, *Fundamentals of Financial Management* (Stamford: Cengage Learning Publishing, 2002), 61.

13. 2008/2009 president of the National Association of Black Accountants Inc.—Nashville, Tennessee Chapter.

more importantly, we have to understand that there are penalties for not paying taxes. We all have seen our share of celebrities with tax problems: Rev. Al Sharpton, Joe Francis, Wesley Snipes, and even George Carlin. Hopefully, your name doesn't get added to the list. Yes, paying taxes helps barbers and stylists stay out of trouble. Ms. Smith says that there are also long-term benefits for paying taxes such as qualifying individuals for federal benefits like Medicare and Social Security. As your career and income moves upward, tax consequences will become more of a factor in your overall career plan.[14]

It is worth noting how important it is to report taxes as precisely as possible. It's the accurate statements that provide proof of income when looking to purchase homes and/or bank loans for bigger shops and salons. Barbers and stylists must understand that everyone is an expert in something. So for taxes to be as precise as possible,

---

14. Xavier Frascogna and Lee Hetherington, *This Business of Artist Management* (New York: Billboard Books Publishing, 2004), 70.

we need to hire specialists to avoid overlooking the small things when it comes to preparing taxes. Tallying up receipts, finding trustworthy tax agencies, and coming up with new ways to save money can be a real task. Ms. Smith says that finding a professional tax preparer will ensure that all the deductions available are received. When tax season comes around, it's always better when money is coming in, not going out. To make the tax preparer's job easier, it is our responsibility to keep good records throughout the year so that the tax preparer can identify the best tax-deductible expenses for our hard-earned profits.

As your business or clientele grows, another advantage of having a professional tax preparer is that he/she will be able to accurately identify new rules that may be overlooked when self-preparing taxes. For example, a tax preparer can determine if you should switch to a different business structure, which would help you take advantage of the most favorable tax treatments.

To maximize the accuracy of our tax statements, we must save as many receipts throughout the year as possible: clipper receipts, uniforms, shampoo, shop equipment, shears, magazine subscriptions, hair show tickets, gas receipts when going to the hair show. Save receipts for anything done that can be related to your profession. These steps will help ensure that taxes are properly completed.

The question still remains, when should taxes be paid? The deadline to pay taxes is April 1 of each year. As far as timetables are concerned, barbers and stylists do have the option of paying taxes monthly, quarterly, or annually. Ms. Smith suggests that paying taxes quarterly is perhaps the best method. When taxes are paid quarterly, the amount owed does not appear to be insurmountable. Paying taxes quarterly actually makes the amount owed seem more bearable. The amount will still be the same, but paying four smaller payments versus one large lump sum at the end of the year has its advantages; it is not so overwhelming. If you choose to pay quarterly, the four payments are due April 15, June 15, September 15, and January 15.

Again, tax is a complicated subject with an infinite amount of topics. Fortunately, there are several Web sites that can help bring more clarity as new questions arise. The IRS Web site (www.irs.gov), for example, has tax tables to help individuals know how much to pay. Visiting IRS's Web page can also show you how to avoid problems in the future by taking steps to rectify past problems.[15] In addition, most forms and explanations of forms can be found on IRS's Web page. To obtain forms not available on the Web site, call (800) 829-3676. IRS can answer just about any question imaginable. The Small Business Administration (www.sba.gov) is also a good resource for assisting with small businesses' questions. Following the steps of this section plus a little Web site research will help minimize the difficulties of tax season.

---

15. Xavier Frascogna and Lee Hetherington, *This Business of Artist Management* (New York: Billboard Books Publishing, 2004), 70.

Create a Budget

Why are budgets so important? One reason: success and budgets work hand in hand. Budgets help give life to visions. In other words, success welcomes budgets. A budget ensures that financial arrangements needed are in place to accomplish goals that have been set. Simply put, a budget is a financial road map.[16] Since money comes and goes, creating a budget is the first stage of attempting to spend money wisely.

Consider how important gasoline is as a means of transportation. We all know that gasoline is used to fuel cars and airplanes; however, no matter how specific drivers' or pilots' plans are to reach their destination, the vehicle will not move without fuel. Fuel is the energy that propels a vehicle. A plan is great but insignificant without the energy needed to put the plan in motion. As fuel is to transportation, budgets are to plans. Budgets fuel ideas. When

---

16. Xavier Frascogna and Lee Hetherington, *This Business of Artist Management* (New York: Billboard Books Publishing, 2004), 70.

managed correctly, budgets bring life to goals. So a living budget is important because it gives vision to exactly where funds will come from and, better yet, illustrates how to allocate funds in all situations.

Budgets help to manage circumstances. Since there are thousands of life scenarios, there are many methods for creating budgets as well. The one most effective for barbers and stylists is the Percentage of Profits approach. You'll usually hear this method often stated as "Our promotion budget for this year is x percent of last year's net profits."[17] This is an effective method to use because you will know exactly where funds will come from and how much will be allocated based on the previous year's profits as you set out to accomplish future goals.

After determining how much to apply to specific areas, create a full list of what will be budgeted. For example, most small-business owners consider payroll taxes and benefits, training (hair shows, etc.), advertising, shop supplies, rent

17. Eric Berkowitz et al., *Marketing* (New York: McGraw-Hill/Irwin Publishing, 2003).

expense, maintenance, tool supplies, utilities, security expense, insurance, shop taxes, professional fees, pest control, market research, credit card fees, tax agency fees, depreciation, furniture expense, shop equipment expense, miscellaneous, toiletries, and magazine subscriptions. This is a simplified list. Know that every person's budget will vary. You have to be creative enough to capture the essence and nature of your shop in your own budget. This approach takes time. You may have to delete and/or develop budget items quarterly, monthly, and weekly or all the time. Creating a budget is an evergreen process.

Once you create budget items that capture your business's specific needs and manners, prioritize them. This is important because financial situations change throughout the year or even from month to month. There are times when we are very busy and others when business slows down considerably. Just think about how incoming money differs according to specific times of the year. Some months or quarters are better for barbers and stylists than others. For most of us, the fourth quarter of the year usually has more customer traffic than the first quarter. The reason—the fourth quarter has more holidays: Columbus Day, Halloween, Election Day, Veteran's Day, Thanksgiving, Christmas, Kwanzaa, and New Year (to name a few). HINT: These and all holidays are marketing opportunities for your business. Review key 6 if needed. Anyway, a budget will help balance busy months and quarters with slower months and quarters of the year. When needed, we have to be able to make adjustments in our budgets to account for high and low points of the year without losing focus of why we have a budget in the first place—to fuel our visions. We do this by aligning budget items into three categories: (1) investments, (2) credit/bills, and (3) living expenses. This way, when budget cuts are necessary, you know where and how to fine-tune your budget.

It is important to realize that there are three levels of hierarchy in a budget. Of the three, the investment category is the highest level. Highest meaning "should not be tampered with regardless of what life throws our way." The investment category holds the highest rank; therefore, it is the most valued group of the budget items. Our investments set us up for future successes. Because this section is comprised of golden future nest eggs, this section of your budget should never be compromised. These items help propel your future and should never be adjusted. Investment items are things that go up in value such as the shop mortgage. This is the last thing you do not pay. Always pay investment items on time. In the future, you will be able to pull money from your investments to fund other projects. So items in this category are highly treasured.

The credit/bills category is another group that must be given specific attention. The credit/bills section is the second tier. This group is important because our debts must be paid in order to maintain good credit. Hopefully, when things are good and you have been able to stabilize life's situations by maintaining a good budget, you can pay more on the debts that you owe. If needed, this group can be adjusted as life situations change. Say, you have an equipment bill for $100 a month and you are short each month during the slow part of the year. It is better to pay into the investment category even if you have to pay a little less in the credit/bills category until things change for the better. Making sure the shop's mortgage is paid is very important. It is important to separate items into the right groups so that when cuts are needed, you know what is important.

The third section of a well thought-out budget is the living expense section. Items in this section are the first to change when adjustments are needed. In a make-believe world, a budget is never altered; but in the real world, change is ever present. As you go through a spell when incoming funds are vanishing quicker than you can pay bills, pay less on items in this section when needed. If you are short $100 a month, it is better to get your cable bill readjusted for less service or to get it temporally disconnected rather than to pay $100 less on your mortgage. The reason a budget is broken into three sections is to ensure that bills remain prioritized. It also provides order when things seem to get hectic. Managing your budget no matter what life throws at you points toward one direction—success.

The chart below is a simplified illustration of how to allocate each need into the correct subdividers of a budget: investments, credit/bills, and living expenses.

Figure 7

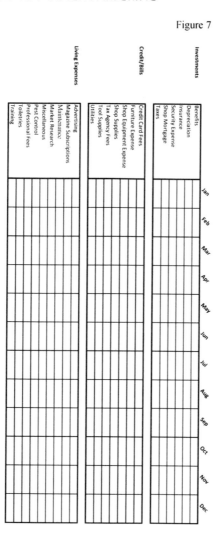

91

Go Forth and Conquer

Key 8

Aspiration.

If the previous seven keys are applied correctly, with your barber or stylist skills, you should stand out among other barber-stylists in your community. Unfortunately, skills alone will not push you to exceed standards. A desire to overcome obstacles must become a part of your makeup. Extraordinary professionals always *will* themselves away from an average crowd of ordinary people. We have to be highly motivated if we expect to succeed. We have to work hard to separate ourselves from the pack. Since you have read this far, you actually should be equipped with the keys necessary to succeed. Will you use the keys to create a lasting career for yourself, or will *you* stand in your own way? Will you use the keys to unlock your successful career?

Success will not wrestle with us. Victory will not come until we recognize that we are often our own biggest obstacles. It will simply move on to barbers and stylists that are willing to make the adjustments needed to become strong willed. We have to realize that sometimes we need help. To find success with as few complications as possible, we barbers and stylists must find a mentor to help us navigate around future struggles. We must also figure out a way to not become our own stumbling blocks.

Find a Mentor

Around the corner of every decision made is a pitfall that awaits us. Fortunately, through mentors we can avoid problems that may otherwise seem difficult and hard to handle. A mentor is a wise, trusted, influential, and seasoned person who can help guide those with less experience down a road the mentor has already traveled. Some of us like learning the hard way, but most of us need a mentor.

I remember sitting in barber school on slow days thinking, *This is for the birds. Next year, when I get out of here, I'm gonna be busy every day.* Optimistic, yes, but unrealistic. I told one of my instructors. He giggled and said, "If it's slow in here, it's slow out there as well." After I graduated from barber school, what do you think happened? I ran into a few slow days, to say the least. Fortunately, I remembered the conversation with my mentor. So I waited out the slow days and learned quickly the up-and-down cycles of the business. I often see new barbers and stylists that have problems understanding this simple principle— not all days are busy days. Luckily for me, I learned to be patient sooner than later. I credit this veteran understanding to mentorship.

Sometimes mentors are unaware that others lean on them for understanding. My instructor in barber school had no idea that I looked upon him as a mentor. However, most mentors are aware that we lean on them for growth. Most of my mentors came from just asking questions especially when I am around barbers that have been in the industry longer and have more understanding. I have found that genuine barbers and stylists look forward to sharing their experiences—good or bad—with upcoming barbers and stylists.

A mentor is important because his or her hindsight can become your foresight. This is significant since hindsight explains the injuries that foresight will prevent. There is no need for us to struggle through what others have already gone through. Since no one has gone through everything, everyone needs a mentor. All of us have room to grow and should seek out alliances that lean toward mentorships. Mentorship helps improve the industry. A better industry is created because over time, more barbers and stylists will avoid mistakes that will be foreseen. As a result, barbers and stylists that advance because of mentorships will most likely become mentors in the future as well. So no matter how many pitfalls await us, danger is not so troublesome as long as we are guided by trusted individuals, friends, and mentors. Others can make suggestions that point us toward success, but what do we do when that is not enough?

Stumbling Block?

Even after finding someone to help us handle unforeseen situations, we still have to make moves (ourselves) that lead toward success. Mentors will lay out different scenarios for different situations, but ultimately, we have to choose the correct paths to find the best result no matter the circumstances. So the only true thing that can truly stand in the way of our accomplishments is our own selves.

When things don't go the way we dream, often we blame others. No matter if we blame others, live in the past, or procrastinate, we are often the instruments of our own disappointments.

To be an exceptional barber-stylist, failure cannot be a part of your formula for success.

Strategies must be adopted to combat frustrations. Be straightforward with yourself: always be proactive, live in the *now*, do not fear failure, avoid negative thinkers, be goal oriented, and learn to embrace change.

According to *Merriam-Webster*, being proactive means to act in anticipation of future problems, needs, or changes. Because proactive people think ahead, they usually reach success first. They think of how to deal with future situations now. To illustrate, did you save up money monthly to renew your license, or did you scramble at the last minute to come up with the fees? If you saved over time, you had a proactive strategy. Proactive people never wait for things to happen and then adjust. No one can think of everything, but proactive people at least try to plan ahead. Being proactive helps you save time and money, but more importantly, it helps you stay stress free. This is important because the more you are free from stress, the more time you have to think of ideas that help separate you from the pack.

When a barber-stylist is not proactive, he or she will struggle through life and miss many opportunities that lead toward success. Always search for solutions and shortcuts to make life as a barber-stylist easier.

There is no gift more precious than the present. Of course, yesterday was a gift but it is now stuck in the past and tomorrow will also be a gift but we may or may not see it. The one true gift we have is today. We must learn to cherish today and take full advantage of now. We are certainly endowed to yesterdays and tomorrows because they give us opportunities to study the past and plan for the future. Although they help us study and give us opportunities to plan, today is still the most important day of our life. It is the only time we truly have to make things happen. Today gives us the opportunity to put action to yesterday's plans. Today also gives us the opportunity to be proactive toward future opportunities and/or problems. When we put off today's action items until tomorrow, we transfer today's energy and power to tomorrow. The problem here is tomorrow is not promised.

Leaders never sit around; they never procrastinate. Leaders make things happen (today). If you are a barber or stylist looking to separate yourself from others in your community, learn to take advantage of today. Taking advantage of today is the easiest area to break away from other barbers and/or stylists. Try doing what you planned each day for a month. Take full advantage of every day that you wake. Go ahead and send the e-mails you planned on sending your customers. Go ahead and restock your products today. Call your vendors to see if you can get your products in early. Call your corporate accounts; as a matter of fact, make cold calls for possible new corporate accounts. During downtime, clean your clippers, sharpen your shears. These are the things barbers and stylists intend on doing. To tell the truth, all barbers and stylists have good intentions, but the few that actually attack action items become leaders in their local communities. They go to the head of the pack by simply taking advantage of today.

We should take advantage of the entire day each day that we are blessed to see. Actually, it is of most importance to live in the now in all areas of our lives, not just the few hours that we are barber-stylists.

The one thing that stops people from taking full advantage of their days is a fear of failing. How do you look at fear? Most barber-stylists are unclear of how to use fear on their roads toward success. Fear often has a negative undertone, but it is actually more constructive than we think. Fear is an emotion that humans use as a survival tool. Fear is essential because it helps us steer clear of dangers and hazards. Now the fear of failing is what we must stay away from; it hinders us from having productive days. Fear is helpful, but the fear of failure is an enemy of success. It is the enemy of creative growth. It steals ambition, enthusiasm, and self-discipline. The fear of failure also obstructs opportunities. This is a dilemma because as barber and beauty entrepreneurs, we cannot fear failing at opportunities that present themselves to us, knowing that opportunities lead toward success. Most of the time, things we fear (such as the fear of failing) are in our minds and are merely barriers we have to learn to overcome. Since we have control of our minds, we can overcome this unconstructive fear. To alleviate the fear of failing, we must (1) make a habit of trying new things and (2) become experts at stepping outside the box. In actuality, if we fail or not, the more we try new things, the closer we are to becoming successful. So there is actually an encouraging side to failing. Ask any successful barber-stylist or your mentor; I'm sure nearly all will say that their failures quickly became their teachers. Therefore, on our roads to success, we must also welcome failures as friends and teachers. So failure is okay; it's the fear of failure we must learn to avoid.

We must also steer clear of people that are scared to step outside the box. It doesn't matter: friends, family, coworkers, church members, or social club members—if they hinder your success, steer clear of them. Yes, beware of people who are scared to fail. Their way of thinking can become contagious, especially since birds of a feather flock together. So avoid negative thinkers. They cannot overcome the fear of failing, and you cannot afford to get stuck in that rut. The fear of failure will always keep average barber-stylists in a box. If you have plans of becoming an exceptional barber-stylist, you have to always think outside the box and constantly try new things. So be clear of this— *never fear failing.*

Now that we know that fearing failure is not an option, we have to make the most of our ideas. We make the most of ideas by setting goals. Goals help ensure that we have a structured plan for reaching success. To illustrate, let's say you want to purchase a new shop or salon next year. The cost is $6,000. In this case, you have to set a goal based on a time line and the amount you can save over a specific period. If you want to purchase the new shop in a twelve-month time frame, you would have to set a goal to save $500 a month ($6,000/12 months). This translates to $125 a week or $25 a day. Now a $25-a-day goal seems more reasonable or within reach than a $6,000 goal. Most of the time we want to investment in opportunities but have no goals set to help us see how we can take advantage of the visions that come our way. Become a goal-oriented barber-stylist and set yourself apart from others by using the SMART [18] goal system:

1. *Specific.* A specific goal has a much greater chance of being accomplished than a general goal. To set a specific goal you must answer the six *W* questions: who, what, where, when, which, and why.
   - o Example: A general goal would be to "build clientele." But a specific goal would say, "I am going to give out twenty business cards a week."

2. *Measurable.* Establish criteria for measuring progress toward the attainment of each goal you set. Measuring your progress helps you stay on track of target dates.

---

18. Gene Donohue, *Top Achievement*, Simpsonville, South Carolina, http://www.topachievement.com/smart.html.

o   To determine if your goal is measurable, ask questions such as, How much? How many? How will I know when it is accomplished?

3. *Attainable*. Figure out ways to make your goals come true.

    o   You will attain goals when you plan your steps wisely and establish a time frame that allows you to carry out those steps. Goals that may have seemed far away and out of reach eventually move closer and become attainable.

4. *Realistic*. A goal must represent an objective you are *willing* and *able* to work toward. You are the only one who can decide just how high your goal should be. Your goal is probably realistic if you truly *believe* it can be accomplished.

5. *Timely*. A goal should be grounded within a time frame. With no time frame tied to it, there's no sense of urgency. If you want to buy a new shop, when do you want to buy it by? "Someday" won't work. However, if you anchor it within a timeframe, "by May 1 of next year," then you've set your unconscious mind into motion to begin working on the goal.

6. T *can also stand for "tangible."* A goal is tangible when you can experience it with one of the senses: taste, touch, smell, sight, or hearing. When your goal is tangible, you have a better chance of making it specific and measurable and thus attainable.

It does not matter how much we plan nor does it matter if we have effective days if we cannot learn to transform with life as it moves. Nothing in life is constant but change. It happens regardless if we want it to or not. The sooner we accept change, the better off we'll live. We have to also learn to avoid becoming our own stumbling blocks by embracing change. Change is a force that's hard to resist. Barbers and stylists that fight change get left behind.

Conclusion

I know you are a good barber-stylist looking to become better because you have just read this book. Now that you have read the *8 Keys to Master Barbering*, commit to memory the principles. Learn to intertwine the principles into your day-to-day operations. Once sunken in, the principles will take you to the next level. Many barber-stylists will never reach full potential and that's okay, but now that you have read the *8 Keys to Master Barbering, you* should become *the* example for success in your community. Use the keys to unlock every door and turn all opportunities into successes. Once you unlock doors that held you back in the past, you will have more space to tackle opportunities and more legroom to work toward victories. Just remember that success is always behind locked doors, and it's your job to use the keys to unlock your opportunities. Use the principles in the *8 Keys to Master Barbering* to separate yourself from competition.

Remember to always:

- use your skills to boost the confidence of customers,
- intertwine your clientele's talents with other customers' needs,
- know who you are in the scheme of your local economy,
- always keep a clean shop,
- sell products that are sensible and reasonable for your clients,
- never let your tools become outdated,
- understand taxes,
- develop and maintain a healthy budget,
- use surveys to learn the true identities of your consumers, and
- use the traditional and nontraditional methods of marketing.

By completing this book, you have just applied complex principles to your business tool belt. This book lists step-by-step processes that are intended to advance your career. As you apply the principles, you will become busier by the day. As you become busier, you will probably forget some of the principles as time passes. It is proven that we can only retain so much information for specific periods of time. Since that's the case, I suggest rereading this book every six months. But for now, apply the *8 Keys to Master Barbering* to your day-to-day operations and go forth and conquer!

Speaking Engagements

To set up speaking engagements for your barbershop, beauty salon, or barber or cosmetology school, make requests at

8keystomasterbarbering.com

or

8keystomaterbarbering@yahoo.com

Bibliography

Berkowitz, E., Steven Hartley, Roger Kerin, and William Rudelius. *Marketing.* New York: McGraw-Hill/Irwin Publishing, 2003.

Brigham, Eugene. *Fundamentals of Financial Management.* Stamford: Cengage Learning Publishing, 2002.

Donohue, Gene. *Top Achievement.* Simpsonville, SC. http://www.topachievement.com/smart.html.

Dornbusch, Rudiger, Stanley Fischer, and Richard Startz. *Macroeconomics.* New York: McGraw-Hill/Irwin Publishing, 2001.

Frascogna, Xavier and Lee Hetherington. *This Business of Artist Management.* New York: Billboard Books Publishing, 2004.

Hopkins, Tom. *How to Master the Art of Selling.* New York: Warner Books Edition Inc. Publishing, 1982.

Little, Steven S. *The 7 Irrefutable Rules of Small Business Growth.* Hoboken: John Wiley & Son Publishing, 2005.

O'Sullivan, Arthur. *Urban Economics.* New York: McGraw-Hill/Irwin Publishing, 2003.

Notes

CPSIA information can be obtained at www.ICGtesting.com
Printed in the USA
BVOW01s2301090614

355911BV00001B/139/P